Thank y
Kenny.

The Devil Wears A Kitchen Apron

by

Kenny Wilson

Kenny The Chef – The Social Poet

Copyright

© 29th April 2024, The Devil Wears A Kitchen Apron. Author Kenny Wilson: Kenny The Chef – The Social Poet.

All rights reserved. No part of this publication may be reproduced, distributed, or transmitted in any form by any means, including photocopying, recording, or other electronic methods without the prior written permission of the author, except in the case of brief quotations embodied in reviews and certain other non-commercial uses permitted by copyright law.

ISBN: 9798321616093

First printed in England, May 2024.

Dedication

**The sun now follows me,
My grey days have gone away.
Since I found you, everything is more than okay.**

To my little Kiwi

CONTENTS

INTRODUCTION 1
TRUE REFLECTION 4
WAR ZONE 7
"CHECK ON" 8
USE BY DATE 10
ONE FOR THE ROAD 11
INGREDIENTS 14
DOG BREATH ON MY FACE 16
MA'AM 20
BRIGHTLY COLOURED WELLIES 23
WILD GARLIC 24
SOMETHING FOR THE WEEKEND 25
ALL ABOUT ME 27
LET THEM EAT CAKE 29
HEAVEN AND HELL 32
BESTIE 35
DIVORCE 37
ARE YOU DEAF OR WHAT? 41
I DREAM OF LIGHT 42

NEANDERTHAL	43
TW@T IN A WHITE HAT	44
ALL ABOUT YOU	46
I FEEL LIKE CHICKEN TONIGHT	47
SICK NOTE	49
HELPING HAND	52
SPICE	54
KNOW THE SCORE	57
R.I.P CATERING TRADE	60
HOLIDAY SKIES	61
HOLDING BACK THE SANDS	62
CALL YOURSELF A MAN?	63
DON'T BE ALARMED	65
TWELVE PENCE	67
AS I STAMMER WITH MY IMPERFECT GRAMMAR	70
PIRATE	71
CHEF CAKE	72
ACKNOWLEDGEMENTS	74

INTRODUCTION

With over 45 years spent in hospitality, I've seen it all. I've met some very interesting people on this journey, working in some of the most demanding establishments from 5-star Scottish hotels, luxury cruise liners touring the world and cooking for royalty, to flipping burgers during covid lock down. I also reached the dizzy highs of working for the BBC and STV (Scottish TV) where I presented cookery programs for some years and wrote food columns for national magazines. Unfortunately, kitchens draw in people with lots of social problems, from which I took some of my inspiration for my street poetry / spoken word / ramblings.

It's an industry where long hours, stressful and hot conditions mixed with social issues, alcohol, drugs and the like make an interesting lifestyle and working environment. This book contains stories and poems about the pressures of working in kitchens, and also the impact it can have on your family life and on yourself.

Us chefs have to balance working long days and holding down relationships and, as you will read, it doesn't always go well. This book contains strong language and references to alcohol, drugs and domestic violence among other things.

To quote James A. Owen:

"All stories are true. But some of them never happened."

I recommend reading my poems / stories out loud to feel the emotions and passion with which they are written.

LOVE KENNY

Dante missed out the kitchen when he spoke about the 9 circles of Hell.

TRUE REFLECTION

Who's that old guy looking at me?

Him there! Can't you see?
White hair and reading glasses,

Neck skin all loose and looking saggy.
Who's the old guy walking with a swagger?
Looking like a drunken version of Mick Jagger.
Oh wait! Wait a minute!

It's my reflection!
Is that truly me?
What happened to the guy of 25?
He's gone in a blink of an eye.

A rebel without a fucking clue!
Not 100% sure of what he wanted to do!
Here stands an image of an old man!
Hands broke from years of chopping,
Knees gone from too much bopping.

Body aches and dreams forgotten,
Wanting to be the next Johnny Rotten.
Bollocks now swing like a grandfather clock!
There's an image you're not going to block.

So where did the time go?
Did someone set my life to fast flow?
Does anyone know? If so, say so!
Is life really that mean?
Or have I been far too keen?

Then I smile and start to remember
The amazing times, the amazing adventures.
Yes, I'm old and grey and saggy.
Each facial line tells a different story.
Mind, not all of them finished in a blaze of glory.

However, I've lived those adventures,
Okay! One that might not be played by the likes of Harrison Ford!
But I was definitely no council schemey bore.

This is the eleventh hour,
My Alamo.
And yes, my time is nearly up,
So, I'm not going to lie,
It's been one hell of a ride.

So, when you see that person in the mirror,
Salute them because they truly are a reflection of you,

And an absolute winner.

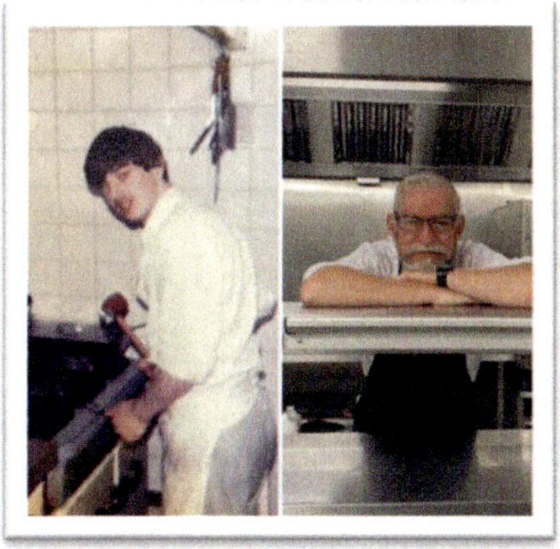

WAR ZONE

Sweat pours from every pore,
Uniform sticks to your body like glue,
Like being cling-filmed, suffocating you,

Heart rate increases, anxiety concerns,
Hands covered in cuts and burns.
I'm tired, fatigued, at a point of no return.

Blood pressure soars,
I'm facing a different type of tour.
One not in the brochure.

This isn't a war zone deployment,
It's my place of employment.
Hospitality in a hostile environment.

Food orders fired like ammunition,
In these roasting hot conditions.
Working in a kitchen you need more than an addiction.

While others sit, eat and relax
I'm feeling like I'm having a heart attack.
Running on empty, that's what us chefs do!
The people out there just don't have a clue
Our tour of duty just to feed you.

"CHECK ON"

"Check on!"

Another food order.
The kitchen goes quiet, that's an order.
Anticipation bites, no natural light,
First class ingredients need to be cooked just right.

Dead animals sizzle in nonstick pans,
The constant whining of extraction fans.
Pieces of food art, placed precisely on a plate
While some rich bloke enjoys his second date.

Sauces and tempers start to simmer.
All this while he eats his overpriced dinner.
Celebrity chef? You're having a laugh!
If he's on the telly,

Who's cooking the guy's £55 sous vide pork belly?
Anxiety in a roasting hot box.
People screaming toxic commands,
flames licking around your hands.

Kitchen filled with fire and smoke.
This place really is a fucking joke.
Minimum wage food artist grabs a quick fag.
No time for that mate!

You're having a laugh!
Bodies tired with cuts and burns.
Don't moan, son! You know the score!
Another chef walks, you need to fill in!

Time off with the family in the bin.
Christmas, birthdays, bank holidays too!
Time off - are you a fool?
Fourteen hours straight without a break,
Have a sniff of this son!
Now get back in and cook them Wagyu steaks.
Life as a chef isn't all that bad,
As long as you're a pyromaniac, single psychopath.

In Dante's Inferno he wrote,
"The devil is not as black as he is painted."
He was right!
Cause sometimes he wears a kitchen apron.

USE BY DATE

Allergens:
Drugs, alcohol, social misfit, unsociable hours, substance abuse.

Use by: 25/12/24

ONE FOR THE ROAD

A family tipple, to celebrate, said mum.
Such a good buzz, such good fun,
Is there any chance of another one?

Cider swigging while hanging with my mates,
Too pissed to climb over the locked park gates.
Standing swaying in front of an angry mum,
Saying to her and the policeman,

"I swear I only had the one!"

Party hard, my badge of honour,
Party clown! "Guilty, your Honour".
Singing songs, kicked out the bar,
"Made it ma! Top of the world." Well, so far!

That's it, I'm done! This is definitely the last one.

I tried to cut down a bit, so I went to an AA meeting with my Mrs, but it was shit.
I came home all depressed and had
a cheeky one from the stash from under my desk.

Then my mates call "Are you coming out for one?"
Going for one? Where's the fun!
You don't even go to an arty farty party and have just one!

A round each, there's 4 done!
"I'm just popping out with my mate's love,
Won't be long. I'm only going for one".

That's it, I'm done! This is definitely the last one.

Me and my girl fell out over my drinking.
She said we need to talk!
It's time to call time, for the sake of our son.
God that really hurt.

"Let's keep it civil," she said!
"Let's sit down and share my special
Birthday bottle of wine."
I didn't have the heart to tell her

I've already drank her half!
And then I drank mine!
So, what if it was a present from her late mum?

I'll pop out later and buy another one.
How hard can it be to find a
Chateau Mouton Rothschild '89?

That's it, I'm done! This is definitely the last one.

Sacked again. I smell like piss.
Another mattress and relationship I'll miss.
But what a night! Well, what I remember,
You canny beat a three-day bender,

Sorry love, who are you?
You need to go. I've got things to do!
Oh wait! Hair of the dog, a little curer!
Well, it would be rude to ignore her,

"You know it's eight in the morning?" she said!
A nagging clock in my bed is not what I ordered.

That's it, I'm done! This is definitely the last one.

In a hospice bed, not at all that happy,
Bladder's gone so I wear a nappy.
My eyes are yellow, my arse is bleeding.
A little night cap of Valium
and a medical book for some bedtime reading.

At my funeral they all say, what a guy!
Thirty-six - too young to die.
My parents toast their only son,

That definitely was the very last one.

INGREDIENTS

These are the ingredients I use every day.
These are the ingredients I use to get paid.

Purée pea, lemon tea,
Chicken legs, free range eggs,
Lamb, jam, Parma ham.

These are the ingredients I use every day.
These are the ingredients I use to get paid.

Sauerkraut, rainbow trout,
ravioli, guacamole,
Breads, shakes, T-bone steaks.

These are the ingredients I use every day.
These are the ingredients I use to get paid.

Mash, hash, boiled and bashed.
Fries, sides, apple pies,
Mussels, Brussels, veal and teal.

These are the ingredients I use every day.
These are the ingredients I use to get paid.

Tray bake, hake, braising steaks,
Chives, pies, spicy Thai.

These are the ingredients I use every day.
These are the ingredients I use to get paid.

Crepes, ceps, shallots in nets.
Grated lime chopped up thyme.
Minestrone, cannelloni, all Italian to me.

These are the ingredients I use every day.
These are the ingredients I use to get paid.

DOG BREATH ON MY FACE

Dog breath on my face, it's time to get up.
Six o'clock on the dot.
In my house you don't need an alarm clock.
Body tired from last night's service,

The smell of grease lingering in every pore.
Dog sitting impatiently by the door.
First smoke grips my lungs like a clamp,
The air outside cold and damp.

I stare like I'm in a trance.
Chemicals weave their familiar dance,
My morning fix caffeine partner, black and thick,
The only thing now that legally does the trick.

Like a human jump lead, I need the kick.
Nicotine-stained fingers merge with cuts and burns
From kitchen nights now just a blur.
Hand skin so hard Avon would make a fortune,
another reason she asks me not to touch her.

So, the morning walk around the block,
Nearly time for work,
Tick tock tick tock.
Nodding to people you sort of know,
The smell of dog breath also up their nose.

Drizzle clings to my face,
As I daydream of ending this early morning race.
Why can't I be rich or be a clerk?
Nine to five. That'll work.

But here I go! Thirteen hours straight,
Making people's "big day" come true.
"Turning Dreams into Reality"
According to the wedding brochures.
There's a quote for you.

All this while I'm holding on to my relationship!
Trying to keep it together with emotional glue,
Why she's still here I haven't a clue.
Cheffing is a young man's trade, they say. True!
But at my age what else can I do?

Eventually home, too tired to walk the dog,
Partner in bed, housework all done,
It shines in the dark.
It smells of Mr. Sheen, it smells of boredom!
Nothing else to clean.

She's sick of being all alone,
Single parent with a pay packet, she said.
All these years later this still rings in my head.
Once again, what am I to do?

I come home a bit early on Sunday night.
I say, "Let's pop out and grab a pint?"
"No love not on a school night.

Get yourself an early night!"
But for a chef a Sunday is a Friday night!
I go to bed and dream about a normal life.
I dream about having that pint.

My alarm clock is right on cue,
My only day off! She doesn't have a clue.
Would you look at that, it's six o'clock?
Dog breath on my face, it's time to get up.

When the Queen died,
I thought about all the people
that had lost their mum or loved one.
For them, time didn't stop,
and life had to carry on.

MA'AM

No minute silence, just silence.
No National Day of Mourning,
No flags at half-mast.
No uniformed soldiers at arms with upturned firearms,

No historic sonnets,
No flowers being thrown on funeral car bonnets.
No David Beckham willing to queue.
While other celebrities skip it and flip it to you.

Siblings standing in wooden pews,
Not knowing what to do.
Holding hands like they have gone back to being ten.
No squabbling, no fighting - this is supporting time for them.

No more having a personal go!
Today is the hardest blow.
"Mum, he hit me!"
Never to be said again.

Mum. That precious name.
A name dying men scream out on the battlefield as they die in pain.

The name you shout out as a kid in the middle of the night,
As you wake from nightmares with such a fright.
Mum. That precious name.
This was our ma'am, our queen, our monarch.

The woman that served us for all those years.
The woman that shed blood, sweat and tears.
The woman that quenched all our fears.

That dealt with scuffed knees while juggling two jobs,
Cooked our dinners if that wasn't enough!

As they walk towards the light,
St Peter's there with his invites.
Looks like he's about to welcome another,
But this time it's our sacred mother.

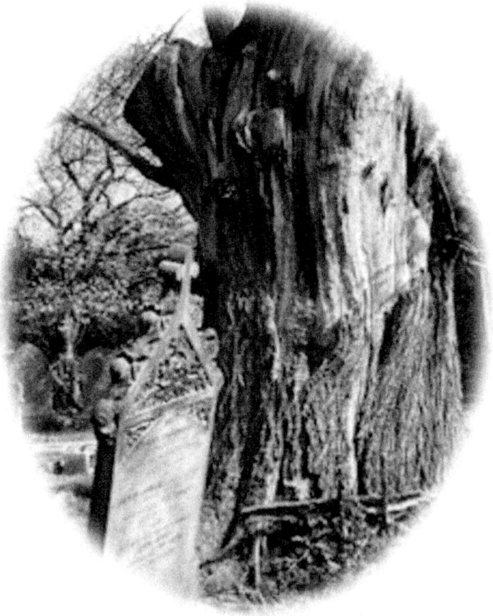

BRIGHTLY COLOURED WELLIES

I want to write a poem that they'll air on the telly.
Something really funny about splashing around in
brightly coloured wellies.
I want to write a poem that fills you full of joy!

Not sadness and disaster,
That makes you cry with laughter.
I want to write a poem about being happy and alive,

That finishes on a high.
Not standing in a kitchen as my life passes me by.
I want to write a poem about splashing around in
brightly coloured wellies.

WILD GARLIC

Wild food for the soul,
Poetry for the mind,
For me they're two of a kind.

SOMETHING FOR THE WEEKEND

What's all this about?
Booking your barber online.
What happened to sitting,
Queuing, looking at
Hair magazines full of designs?

I'm too scared to try anything new.

All I want is a short back and sides.
Is it a sin? I'm just wanting a trim.
No long hair in the kitchen.
Don't want the owners bitching,
Being a chef, it can't be a mess.

I'm too scared to try anything new.

Too afraid to try another style,
But what am I to do?
Asking if I want a fade while shaving my neck with a razor blade.
Buzz cut, flat top, number one or two

I'm too scared to try anything new.

What is a buzz cut?
Do I need to join a crew?

I'm too scared to try anything new.

Young boy next to me, asking for a tram line
I suggested Piccadilly.
He says 'Sick man' but I'm feeling fine!
Youth of today don't have a clue!

I'm too scared to try anything new.

'Something for the weekend sir?'
The barber used to ask.
Now I'm offered wax by young guys,
Tattoos and rainbow boots up to their thighs.
What's with the tatts and bob hats?

I'm too scared to try anything new.

As they brush the floor,
I head for the door,
Wondering why I just paid more,
Even with its hot towel pleasure.
Wondering, would the cheaper place do it any better?

Then I catch my reflection on the bus,
Girl next to me says, 'Nice hair'.
I blush.

Quick! Pass me my phone!
I need to download an app!

I can get a new haircut cut by doing that.
Hold the front page! Yes, it's true!

I'm going to try something new.

ALL ABOUT ME

You whispered to me you wanted me.
You spoke on the phone for hours to me.
You texted me that you loved me.
You wanted to marry me.

So why change me?
Mould me?
Turn me into someone that was not me.
My friends all said they didn't recognise me!
No kitchen knife can inflict the scars you left on me.

Thankfully, through all the pain
I am slowly returning to me.
I can slowly start saying
Yes!
This is me.

LET THEM EAT CAKE

Why teach people to cook on minimum wage?
Let them dine on takeaways.
There's no tax on fresh food!
But there is on fast food.
I'll let you work out the maths on that.

Don't teach the population how to cook.
That will give them control.
We don't want them healthy and growing old.

We closed the local shops.
The developers built ten houses on them plots.
Moved the main shops to out of town.
We gave them help and moved the tax band.
It's okay! Daddy owns the land.

To save our blushes we'll get the revenue
back by cutting the buses.
The old can walk, they have nothing better to do!
Don't worry about them cooking
They can't afford the fuel.

Get their shopping delivered by app.
Our children all have shares in that.
Plus, the government gets twenty percent back.
So, what if they don't have smartphones?

Technology is not for the old.
Don't worry about getting staff in the shops.

We've automated the tills that will keep down the bills.
The shareholders will be thrilled.
And then, with all the unemployed,
We'll house them in our damp cold homes,
But make sure they pay their rent,
We don't make money if they're sleeping in tents.

Do not have food banks in the town!
It makes our politicians look like Eton clowns.
Tax the food banks, that's what we'll do.
There can be no competition the shareholders will not approve.

Keep the people happy by running farmers' markets
Selling locally grown olives and dried fruit from the Bahamas
Don't show the children how to make simple things like soups!
Let's keep them in this controlling loop.

Let the poor eat cake -
But do not teach them to bake.
Marie Antoinette stuck her neck out
For making this mistake.

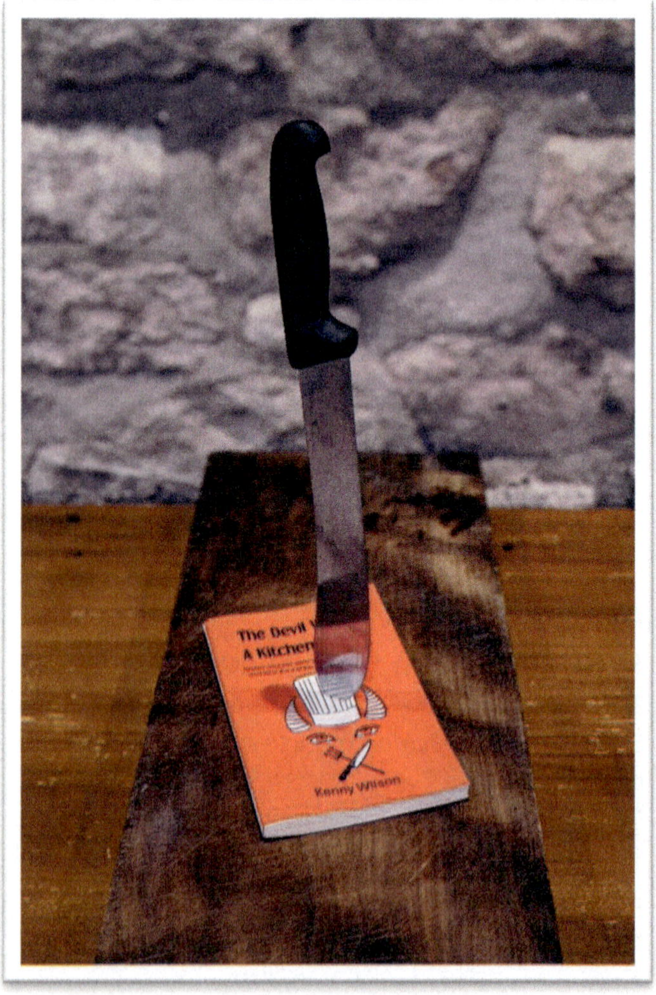
The Devil
A Kitchen
Kenny Wilson

HEAVEN AND HELL

I don't believe in heaven or hell.
I'm sorry if you don't want to hear this,
And if you're a person of the cloth, bear with us
and let me explain.

See, I don't believe in going to heaven
sitting around playing a harp on white fluffy clouds.
No after life or reincarnation.
Shame, mind,

I always wanted to be a butterfly
But not a wasp at any cost.
I don't believe in hell either.
Being cast into the abyss, feeling the heat,

Flames licking around your feet.
A good person will live on within us
After they depart this world.
Surely being loved means they have
reached the ultimate destiny!

As people that loved them feel something is
missing in their lives,
A heart wrenching hollowness for our dearly
departed.
Tears of sadness choke up inside us.

Heaven is in our hearts.
That's why it hurts
When people leave us:
This, the ultimate divorce.

No more texting, no more calls,
But you never delete their number off your phone.
Remember love doesn't go away
Even if the person does.

Hell is a place people go
When you try to erase them out of your mind,
Being talked about with a bitter tongue,
Like they had no right to walk this earth
And steal the air we breathe in the first place.

Their narcissist lifestyle comes to an end.
But no man is born evil,
So, ask yourself,
Where, for them, did it all go wrong?

They know before they die
How they will be remembered.
They will make this planet a better place by
departing it.
Then hopefully they won't be remembered at all.

Their Judas image reflects in their dark soul,
And them praying to a God
They never once thought about
For forgiveness in their 11th hour.

Lying on their deathbed
Isn't going to cut it either.
The grim reaper lives inside their soul.
Their hollow life slowly implodes.
Surely sanctuary is within us all!

An inner peace, a sense of calm.
There is no "In the next world."
There is no "In the next life."

This is the final act! No television rewind.
It's very simple:
If you want to be remembered in here
(tap your heart)

Treat people and yourself with respect.
What I'm trying to say is,
Be a kind person now,
Yes, be strong and tall

But don't be sharp.
This way you automatically get a pass
On learning to play the harp.

BESTIE

My best friend had a piss against my neighbour's gate!
No, it wasn't a mistake, and no it wasn't great!
No, sorry - I couldn't wait or blame it on the drink.

Of course, I was left to clean it up!
If I didn't, what would next door think?
To be honest, personal hygiene isn't their thing.
I have to take them to get their haircut.

And showering is a mortal sin.
They always appear uninvited
Almost like magic when I'm making the tea.
No offer to help or cook for me.

Any chance of help with the washing up?
Once again, I'm out of luck.
Then once I've finished and I want to relax
They've claimed my chair without a care,

Sitting watching my telly with a big full belly!
Food for free "that'll do me".
In vain I ask them, "Did you wipe your feet?
And is there any chance of me GETTING MY SEAT?"

I was hoping for a kiss and a cuddle with the wife
But with them sitting in between us staring, it isn't very nice.
My family all think my bestie is really great,
No mention of the neighbour's gate.

You may ask why I put up with them.
That is the million-dollar question, my friend!
But you see, my life would not be complete.
Even though they never wipe their feet.

The evening walk and a beer before dinner,
They never grass on me, so it's a winner.
They say a dog is a man's best friend.
But sometimes she drives me round the bend.

DIVORCE

It wasn't supposed to be this way!
When I said I loved you
I meant forever not just 6331 days.
So that's that, I suppose.

This isn't our big day.
No smiling for the camera,
No buttonhole flowers to remember.
The champagne isn't chilling on ice.

Cinderella isn't recruiting mice.
No need for a seating arrangement,
Brides' family to the left of me,
Jokers to the right,
No more stuck in the middle with you.

The vicar won't make eye contact with you.
The cake is well past its sell-by date too.
So, what are you supposed to do?

No worrying about the best man's speech.
Groom twitching in a bow-tied suit.
Should there be a last dance?
Do I practise on the off chance?

So many questions!
What do you do with a box of photographs?
Do you split them in half?
Are they your friends or are they mine?
Can you have two of a kind?

The dog was the family pet
But suddenly, she's mine.
The in-laws become the outlaws.
At least I don't need to listen to her dad's stories again.
I've heard them so many times I now class the characters as friends.

The only thing that now gets carried over the threshold
Is the shopping with meals for one.
Struggling to make ends meet.
Constant radio love songs to make you greet.

Facebook deletes to keep things neat.
The dining table with an empty seat.
Divorce. A word that carries a social stigma
Even Billy Connolly spelt it instead of saying it even in a whisper.

Now we are just a statement, read out in a family court.
A reference number of a county clerk.

.

I never wanted to be a statistic
But your temper was unrealistic -
Borderline ballistic.

She took the lot! The cutlery set, the colour TV,
Her Jimmy Choo shoes meant more to her than me.
Designer cars, weekend spas.
Are you keeping up with the image so far?
She certainly breeds negativity:
A special skill, a polished ability.
But I was the rich man:
I left with my dignity.

So here I am in the arms of another,
It was always heading that way
After years of fighting with each other.

A race. I knew there would be no winner.

No more together,
No more riding out the stormy weather.
You never get married to separate.

Why would you go through that pain?
It would drive a person truly insane.
And I hope this poem never gets penned again.

Ian Curtis sang,
Love will tear us apart.
Ours got ripped to pieces.

When people are struggling with their mental health, don't prescribe drugs.

Give them a pen or teach them to cook.

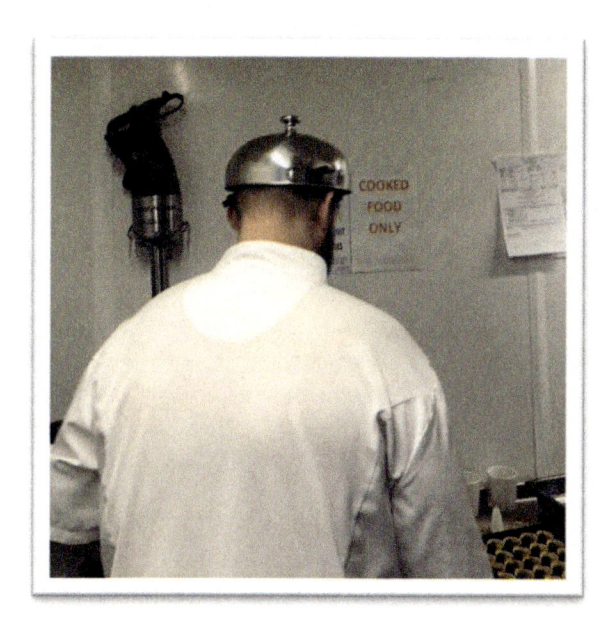

ARE YOU DEAF OR WHAT?

As my hearing erodes my ears are the most important things to me.
If I lost them I would be deaf, but worse, I couldn't see.

"The constant whining of extraction fans".

I DREAM OF LIGHT

The only time I clearly see
is when the night takes me.
I dream of light.
I awake and the darkness returns.

NEANDERTHAL

Cave man chef at his best,
Thinks women should be chained to the sink,
Not interested in what they think!
Just wants them looking pretty in pink,

That's why he's all alone, constantly on his mobile phone,
Swipe left swipe right, every woman gets a fright
Doesn't want a woman in his restaurant kitchen,
Not wanting them to hear his bitching.

Carrying food that's what their meant to do.
Not interested in their points of view.
Thinks every woman wants a screw
Acting the big man and trying to be funny,

Only women that loves him is his Mummy
At her house, he's King of the BBQ
His Language polite, never blue.
Never thought of him as a goody two shoes.

Always drinks bottle beers,
No one must know about his anxiety fears,
Thankfully he's a dying race,
Not a chef just a fucking disgrace.

TW@T IN A WHITE HAT

In what other trade is it acceptable
To wear your burns like a badge of honour?
Blisters and scars mark your arms,
Looking like you self-harm,

Clingfilm-wrapped fingers, knife-torn skin.
Don't cry unless you've lost a limb,
said with a sarcastic grin.
Twelve-hour day,
Works out less than minimum wage.

Would be better off working for Asda.
Head chef tells me that would be a disaster,
"Where's the pride? Where's the passion in that?
You'll look a right twat!"
Does passion pay the bills?

Is the couple on table six paying with passion or
good will?
Or good old-fashioned cash!
Ten percent service charge,
I'll see nothing of that!
Birthday party just booked in,

They want a celebration cake,
"I know you're going on your break,
It's the bosses' mate."

But I'm supposed to be picking up the kids.
They're expecting me at the school gates!
I don't care about time in lieu,

I want to pick the kids up from their school.
My ex is about to get the text.
In capitals she replies,
I HAVE A JOB TOO!

YOU'RE JUST A TWAT IN A WHITE HAT!!
"I FUCKING HATE YOU!"
I write on the cake,
"Happy birthday to you.
I'm screwed whatever I do."

ALL ABOUT YOU

You're maybe not the right one for everyone!

But you're the right one for someone.

That someone will be more important than everyone.

Apart from you.

I FEEL LIKE CHICKEN TONIGHT

I'm not the sharpest knife in the block.
I just found out there's definitely no rat in ratatouille,
No shit in shiitake mushrooms,
No minced-up Toms in the ketchup.

Crudités aren't a collection of naughty words.
I can now stop worrying about them poor people of Alaska getting baked alive.
Thankfully, the Turkish delight has no unwarranted surprise!

Question:
Is a Greek salad in Greece just called a salad?
Asking for a friend!
Eton Mess is very hearty and isn't referring to a political party.
I went to Bakewell for a tart, but all I got was a fat tummy and a broken heart.

Toad in the hole - well that blew my mind!
Something I definitely now won't decline.
I'm obviously gullible, but do the French really eat frogs' legs and snails?
If so, pass me a pail.

Is it also true that they only eat one egg a day?
Is one egg really "un oeuf"?
Spotted dick, passionfruit fool, beautiful Paris
breasts, to name just a few.

All these desserts I can now gladly enjoy and share with you!
Forget the pint of ale, I'm going to wash them down with a sugar pussy cocktail.
I'm obviously not all that bright

But after some research
I'm now happy to eat coq au vin for dinner tonight.

SICK NOTE

It's weird being the same age as old people!
When I meet my mates from our old council estate.
The smell of deep heat,
Wrinkled good looks beating a retreat,
Constant knocking on our doctor's door.

Talking about health issues like a bunch of old bores.
We talk about our tablet combinations!
Where once we wanted to rule the nation,
Now we queue for vaccinations.

Our days of non-prescription drugs
Are well and truly in the past.
No more all-day benders,
Now we struggle to get out the bath.
We talk about our crippled knees,
There's something that we can all agree.

Hands destroyed from years of chopping,
Ears going deaf from clubs long forgotten.
I'm worried my teeth will slip while having a kiss,
And why does it hurt every time I need to take a piss?

NHS on red alert – they've found a lump.

Bend over, sir, this is going to hurt.
"Any chance of a date first, nurse?"
A line that would make any angel curse.

A latex glove and some KY jelly
Why can't I be home watching the telly?
A finger shove is something you can't ignore
And something that you don't really adore.

Asking about my holiday plans
While holding my bollocks in her right hand.
"Cough please" (cough),
This is definitely not going to plan.
I'm sure a few of you can understand.

I now get ready for bed at the same time
I once got ready to go out,
And these days ginger tea is the tipple for me,
But if you insist!
Whisky without the "e" and three ice cubes if you please.

Watching the ten o'clock news is now my new after party,
Wife's Barbie slippers on and a tube of Smarties.

In the morning when I awake
I swing my legs out, and they start to ache.
Brain starts checking to see if everything is still okay.
My mind is still willing but my body's giving up.

Another twenty years with a bit of good luck.

Carpal tunnel, trigger finger too,
A list of illnesses to name a few!
But at my age what am I to do?
Discounted DIY is something I now can do!
But only on Wednesday afternoons – thank you, B&Q.

Just as long as I don't need to bend –
My back has gone once again.
Young shop assistants ask to carry my bags.
This act of kindness makes me flag.

However, I'm not ready to give up
And a medical record is just a shit book.
I'm going to give up talking about being ill
And try taking a few less pills.
I'm going to get fit and exercise a bit!

Maybe stop drinking…. Wait! What?
I'm talking shit.

Cheers. Here's to your ill health and getting old.

HELPING HAND

Life is a big steep staircase!
Every step different.
Some steps steeper than others,
Some feel like you're never going to reach the top!

But look again -
Look where you've got!

Take one step at a time
And don't be afraid to take a little step back.
You're allowed to stop for a bit and breathe.
Just never give up, even when you're on your knees.

But if you look back and see someone else struggling,
Lend them a hand.
As the saying goes, never look down on someone
Unless you're helping them up.
Let me remind you, you were probably there once too,

A helping hand you should never refuse.
No one is exempt from feeling blue.
Respect and equality are a quality all of us should share,

We are humans after all, and yes, we care.
Never feel alone and you can't reach out,

There're angels out there without a doubt.
Help is just a text, a call, an email away.
You'll never be turned away,
No matter what, You have to say.

SPICE

Bride and groom hug me and cry,
Telling me how much they're on a high
I've cooked their perfect dinner,
Everyone's a winner,
Saying I got it perfect on the spice.

Asking me, when I get home, do I cook for the wife?
I don't have the heart to say, that would be nice:
I've been divorced more than twice.
Not what you want to hear on your big day.

I go back to the kitchen and start sharpening my knives.
Better than going home to an empty house,
A house without a spouse.

Telling the kitchen crew
We nailed it on the spice.

The crew are my family:
The ones I say good morning, good evening, and good night to.

I leave an empty kitchen and turn out the lights.
I sneak into my house, quieter than a mouse,

No one there, no one cares.
Everything dark at this hour of night.
At least I can say I got it perfect on the spice.

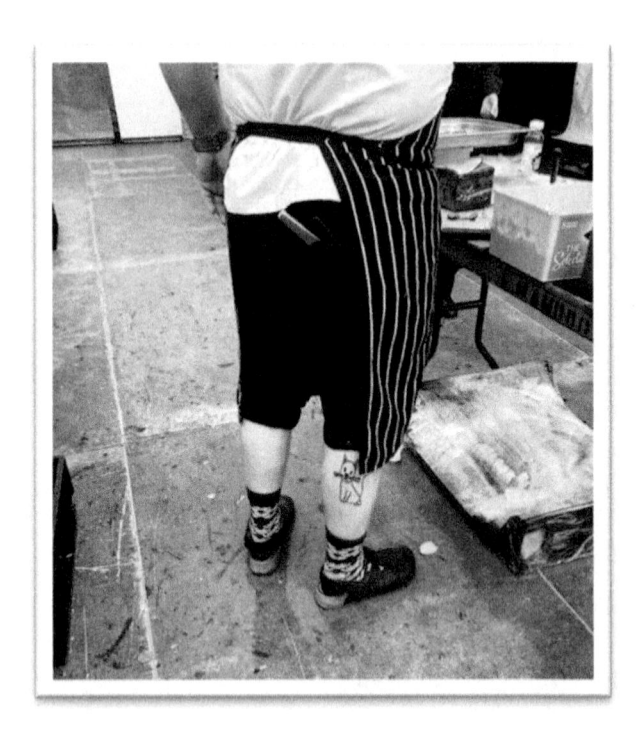

Oh Billy! Why did you have to take your life away?

Was life that grey you had to leave us on Christmas day?

My head waiter in Guernsey - what a brilliant, funny man. RIP my friend.

KNOW THE SCORE

Don't add your name, there's no one else to blame.
Just a social thing he said! no shame.
You can quit whenever you like, it's like riding a bike.
It's going to be a hit! Your mates are all taking it!

Come on, you know the score.

He's everyone's pal, a murderer on speed dial.
"Have one on me, try it for free!"
They're not addictive, ask Harriet or Steve -
They've been on it for years and they have no fears!
A bit of snow with the crew - it would be rude not to.

Come on, you know the score.

A chemical reaction, you never thought it could happen.
Crawling on the piss-stained toilet floor,
Praying to God for less and not more.
You can see the bright light. Let's hope it's just a fright.
Stay away from the light! Stay away from the light!

Come on, you know the score.

Your body's aching, what have you taken?
Temperature soars, "I don't like this anymore."
What have I done? I only took the one!
The blue flashing light, It's definitely not your night.

Come on, you know the score.

Policewoman knocks at the door,
Sister shouts down, "If it's Bridget, I'll be there in a mo."
Dad just stands in silence and listens.

Mum's screaming,
"You've got the wrong house.
You've got the wrong door!
He doesn't touch that stuff anymore."

Come on, you know the score.

All huddled in the rain, mum's crying again.
Priest with dirt-stained hands, preaching that it's Gods will,
He didn't die in vain.
"Ashes to ashes, funk to funky." Don't die like Tom the social junkie.

Come on, you know the score.

Your speed dial pal, trying to fill a hole.
Lost revenue for him the hardest blow.
"Have one on me, try it for free!
It's just a social thing! Trust me!"
All this for some fun, try a week in the sun.
A bit of escapism, try looking after number one!

It is your life! You're right!
But have you ever seen a happy junkie?
No! Neither have I!

The Cranberries sang.
"To all those people doing lines,
Don't do it. Don't do it."
Drugs don't discriminate.
Don't die a social junkie.
Be your own person tonight.

Come on, you know the score!

R.I.P CATERING TRADE

Celebrity chefs killed the catering trade.
An achievement no one else can truly claim.
At sixteen years old,
Would you want to be a chef?
Being told you're not worth a fuck with every breath.

Watching a young chef being slapped
With two bits of bread
Pressed against their vulnerable head.
An idiot sandwich! Treated like a dummy.
Let's all laugh, aye it's funny.

These chefs are only in it for the money.
Their egotist life is a minority of one:
I didn't see anyone else having fun.

Yeah, they can cook, but for everyone else
They don't give a fuck.
Their millions made by their underpaid workers,
Minimum wage staff like lambs to the slaughter.

The next time you see a celebrity chef on the telly,
Remember there's a pour old sod like me behind him,
Getting it all ready.

HOLIDAY SKIES

Nothing beats that first holiday drink.
Sun, making you blink.
Sunburned bum,
Flicking best sellers with your thumb,
Factor 50 Celtic skin,
Free pouring gin,
Warmth within.

Dining al fresco instead of ready meals from Tesco.
Shorts and sandals the dress code.
Fancy another? I guess so!

Enjoying the heat - not like the kitchen!
This one's a treat.
Someone else behind the stoves
Feeding tourists in their droves.

Don't get much on my salary:
Just enough to recharge my batteries.
God, I'm loving eating 3,000 calories.

Being quintessentially British and
Talking about the amazing weather
Hoping this day will last forever.

HOLDING BACK THE SANDS

Our relationship built like a sand sculpture.

Beautiful, unique,
Everyone in awe,
But not even King Canute could hold back
the tide of energy
That would overpower us,
Erasing our foundations.
A tsunami of emotions.

Our castle, our dreams
Now just sand beneath people's feet.

CALL YOURSELF A MAN?

Call yourself a man?
The guys in the kitchen would laugh at you!
Grow a pair, that's what you need to do.
Was this part of the plan?

Allowing a woman to hit her man.
So, what if she bit you in the face?
Cover it up, leave no trace.
It's easier believing it won't happen again,

Too embarrassed to tell your friends that
Domestic violence happens to men.
Walking on eggshells, trying to keep the peace.
No point talking to the police.

The next day she's so, so sorry.
Promising it will never happen again.
Blames it on stress, busy career.
Pours you an ice-cold beer.

How long can you live in fear?
She slips on that little black number,
Takes you by the hand
With tears in her eyes.

How many times can she apologise?
Then she shows you her thighs.
Your dignity dies inside.
Trying to prove you truly are a man,
Brain wondering if it will happen again.
Not a case of it, but when.

Never hit back. Walk away.
Start afresh, don't delay.
Don't believe what they say.
Yes, you can.
And by doing this you truly are a man.

The Office for National Statistics figures show, one in 6-7 men and one in 4 women will be a victim of domestic abuse in their lifetime. Of domestic abuse crimes recorded by the police, 25% were committed against men.

DON'T BE ALARMED

How come
I can't get to sleep.
Fourteen hours on my feet,
Ten days in a row.

Body is tired, old.
Am I losing control?
Brain is like an unruly child,
Running wild.

All day in a kitchen,
But I never eat.
Six coffees is my treat.
My body is hungry,

Brain needs refuelled.
Finally, I fall asleep.
Just in time to hear
The alarm clock go,

Beep beep beep.

Farming is a job up there with cheffing:

Long hours working in the cold and dark. But without farmers we would have no food and I'd have nothing to cook for you.

TWELVE PENCE

Up at four, straight out the door.
Outside it's cold and dark,
Rain coming down so hard.
Wondering if you need to build an ark?

Getting the herd in one by one.
All done before the rise of the sun.
Working a twelve-hour day,
Works out less than minimum wage.

Making 12p for milking the cows!
Tory government, take a bow.
Twelve pence makes no sense,
How are we supposed to pay the rents?

The government say we are supporting our farmers.
By buying cheap fruit and veg from Guatemala!
Supermarket banners saying 'Eat British meat'
While selling New Zealand lamb on the cheap.
Aberdeen Angus that never once grazed our lands,
Yet it was our farmers that faced the export bans.

We are an island and need to be more self-sufficient,
But we are dealing with a government that's so incoherent.
When a farm closes down and

Turns into a rich man's mansion,
Try offering twelve pence to the likes of Richard Branson.

Here's to the government,
Whether this one or the next.
Remember us farmers,
Yes! There's still a few,
And after four years we can sack you!

So, if you want our vote,
No more sitting on the fence.
It's going to cost you a lot more
Than your Judas twelve pence.

Spoken word.

The poetry of the people.

Words for the masses not the upper classes.

AS I STAMMER WITH MY IMPERFECT GRAMMAR

Do I really need to know about iambic pentameter
Or understand caesuras and enjambment?
I write the words from my heart.
That, my darlings, is my art.
I don't rhyme in lines of 4 haiku (hi coo).
I'm obviously not educated like you.

Shakespeare and Byron would call me a ned
As I only write words down as they appear in my head.
As I said, it comes from the heart,
But is this really, truly art?

As I stammer with my imperfect grammar,
I hear them tutting at my lack of tanka.
But this is my propaganda.

Writing isn't a religion,
Not like following a recipe in a kitchen.
I don't care if my work isn't valued,
My literature skills presented like a tossed salad.

Shakespeare, take a bow.
But I prefer Jack and the Beanstalk.
Unfortunately, I cooked the beans along with the coo.

PIRATE

When I finish in the kitchen
That's when I start my drinking,
I don't look on it as an addiction.

My kitchen service is my high
I just need the drink to help get me by.
One or two with the crew.

It's a chef thing - that's what we do,
Like buccaneers, cutthroats, privateers,
By drinking beer, I hide my fears.

"Drinking rum before 10 am makes you a pirate, not an alcoholic."   **- Granger Smith**

CHEF CAKE

1kg of self-raising doubt
A level spoon of tiredness
2tbls of overworked
2tbls of underpaid
150ml of alcohol
100g of tobacco
1/2 tsp of white powder
250g of pressure
250g of leadership
175g of attention to detail
100g of multi-tasking
1/2 tsp of social misfit
1 tsp of sarcasm
4 failed relationships
1 large tbsp of regret
A large pinch of suck it up

Mix all the ingredients together, leave to stand for 13 hours, bake in a hot-tempered oven-type room. Turn out once it looks tired and overdone.
Repeat daily.

Let's Cook

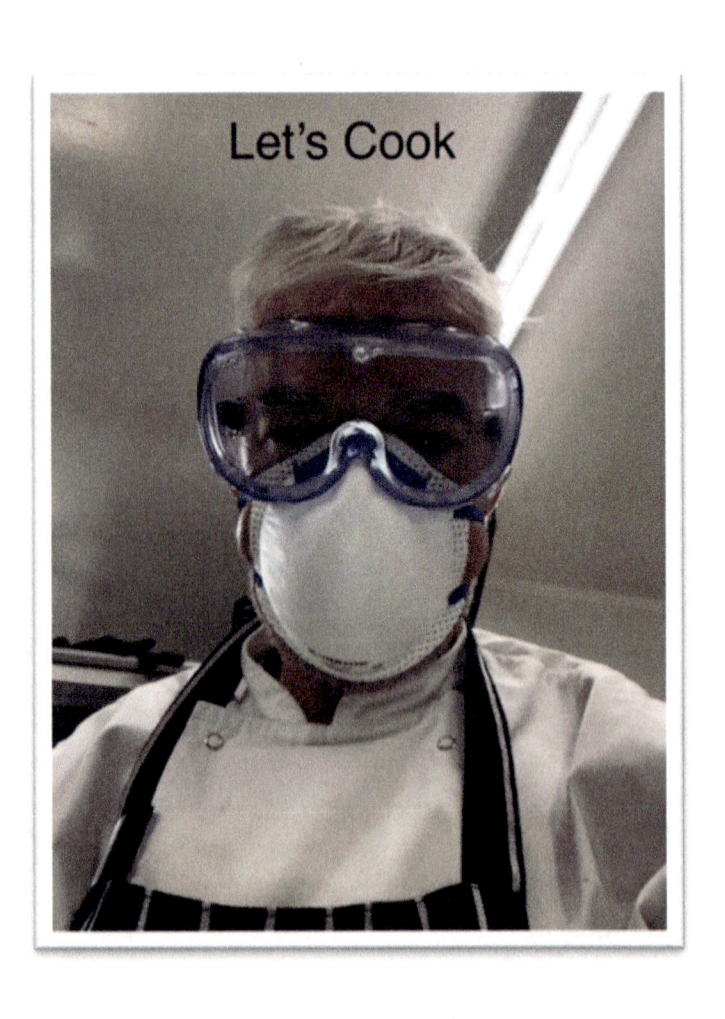

ACKNOWLEDGEMENTS

I never dreamt I could possibly write a book on spoken word or even more get up on a stage and read to an audience, but I did, and I have.

The first thanks go to my amazing children Antonia and Lewis who have always supported me even through the darkest of days; I love you so much. To Kate Wilson (no relation) for editing my ramblings, Danae Mayo for the help with the book cover. Pete Thys for his help with the photography. Jan Riley without her help this book would be still sitting on my computer.

To my closest chef friends Stephen Gilmore and Mick Poole who have shared life and kitchens with me. We have drank, cooked, laughed, and cried together. If you need to look up the definition of friends, you will see their names.

A big thank you to all the chefs that I have worked with; some have inspired me by entering a kitchen, some by leaving it.

To the friends I have gained and lost, for your inspiration I thank you.

Thank you for reading my book. I hope this gives you an insight into the life behind the stoves and the people that work so hard to make your meals so enjoyable. Remember these people are human: they also have issues just like you and are trying their hardest to serve you and doing a job that can be demanding.

These people are passionate about their jobs, so please...

BE KIND!

Instagram @kennythechef_thesocialpoet

Email – kennythechefpoet@outlook.com

If you are in the hospitality trade and struggling with your mental health reach out to these guys:
www.theburntchefproject.com

The Gleneagles Hotel

3 Amigos

Printed in Great Britain
by Amazon